Powered by the Gift of Tongues

PUBLISHER:
Kenneth L Fabbi, Lethbridge, Alberta, Canada
Email: FiveFoldCycle@gmail.com
Copyright © 2023 by Kenneth L. Fabbi

All rights reserved.

Unless otherwise indicated, all biblical quotations are taken from the New International Version (NIV) bible translation.

The Holy Bible, New International Version®, NIV® Copyright © 1973, 1978, 1984, 2011 by Biblica, Inc.® Used by permission. All rights reserved worldwide.

21st Century King James Version®, Copyright© 1994. Used by permission of Deuel Enterprises, Inc., Gary, SD 57237. All rights reserved.

No part of this publication may be reproduced in any form, or by any means, electronical, including photocopying, recording, or any information browsing, storage, or retrieval system, without permission in writing from the Author.

Kenneth would welcome your communication at FiveFoldCycle@gmail.com

ISBN:
Paperback ISBN: 978-1-7771066-1-4
eBook ISBN: 978-1-7771066-2-1

Subjects: Christianity - - Holy Spirit - Growth - - Spiritual Gifts

I. Title   II. Fabbi, Kenneth L.

POWERED BY THE GIFT OF TONGUES

TABLE OF CONTENTS:
Section 1 – Overview   7

It all started at Pentecost   7
Prayer in Tongues defined   8
Paul uses adjectives like desirable and edify   11
Yielding to the Spirit   13
Tongues is always under the control of the individual   14
Here is what some Preachers say about Tongues   15
How does this apply to my life today?   16
Accessing the Rivers of Living Waters   19
An expression of intimacy   21
What about mysteries?   21
Summary   22

Section 2 – Depth   23

We do not understand, so 'what do we do'?   23
The Spirit will teach us   25
We are told by St. Timothy to stir-up the Spirit within   28
The Study of the Phenomena/Gift of Speaking in Tongues – Glossolalia   28
Decreased Brain Activity   30

Section 3 – Scripture   32

Understanding the Gift of Tongues by studying Scripture
How does Tongues manifest?   32
    I. Tongues is a personal prayer   32
    II. Is interpretation necessary?   36
        A. Tongues can be understood by unbelievers (without interpretation - possibly a miracle)   36
        B. Some of the listeners did not understand Tongues   37

      C. Peter recognizes that they are speaking in Tongues 38

III. Tongues is a sign for non-believers 39
IV. The Gift of Tongues used in an assembly 40
    Desirable 40
    Orderly 41
    Edifies 41
V. Summary of the manifestation of Tongues 42

Section 4 – Conclusions 43

Common Misconceptions 43
Tongues is evidence of the Baptism in the Spirit. Partially True 43
Tongue can only be used if it is interpreted. False 47
God will give Tongues to me when he wants. Partially True 48
Tongues only occurs by inspiration. Partially True 49
The Gift of Tongues has ceased. False 52
The Gift of Tongues is not for every believer! False 53
Tongues is just gibberish; they are making it up or imitating. This statement is poorly thought out. 55

Summary 56
I Challenge you 56
A Prayer for the Holy Spirit and the Gift of Tongues 57

Appendix A 58
Prayer For Baptism In The Spirit

Appendix B 60
Course Material taken from *You Can Minister Spiritual Gifts*

Notes 68

ACKNOWLEDGEMENTS:

The draft of this booklet sat around for over a year. During that time, I sent the draft to a number of people to help them understand the Gift of Tongues. I am always interested in the questions and comments that come from these interactions. Many of the topics for the section 'Common Misconceptions', came from these folks. I want to thank you.

Many thanks to the two editors, Karla Conte and Lisa Feser. Your editor's eyes made the material easier to read and eliminated my very bad jargon. It is always amazing to see what you see and receive your input.

Thanks to both of you!

POWERED BY THE GIFT OF TONGUES

Section 1 – Overview

It all started at Pentecost:

> *³ They saw what seemed to be tongues of fire that separated and came to rest on each of them. ⁴ All of them were filled with the Holy Spirit and began to speak in other tongues as the Spirit enabled them.*
> Acts 2: 3-4

The first time we see Tongues mentioned in the Bible is Acts 2: 3-4. It is one of the markers or signs of the empowering of the Holy Spirit.

The Apostles received the Holy Spirit at Pentecost and began to speak in Tongues. The Apostles expect that others who receive the Holy Spirit will exhibit similar signs. For example, in Acts 10, we see this gift of the Holy Spirit poured out on the Gentiles. The Apostles recognize the gift when they hear the Gentiles praying in Tongues and praising God:

> *⁴⁵ (They)... were astonished that the gift of the Holy Spirit had been poured out even on Gentiles. ⁴⁶ For they heard them speaking in tongues and praising God.*
> Acts 10: 45-46

You and I are Gentiles and therefore open to receiving the Gift from the Father, which is His Holy Spirit.

The Apostles also recognized that baptized people did not have the Holy Spirit. In Acts 19, a group of twelve baptized believers in Ephesus receive the gift when Paul laid his hands on them.

> [3] *So Paul asked, "Then what baptism did you receive?" "John's baptism," they replied.* [4] *Paul said, "John's baptism was a baptism of repentance. He told the people to believe in the one coming after him, that is, in Jesus."* [5] *On hearing this, they were baptized in the name of the Lord Jesus.* [6] *When Paul placed his hands on them, the Holy Spirit came on them, and they spoke in tongues and prophesied.* [7] *There were about twelve men in all.*
> Acts 19: 3-7

The experience of the Gift of Tongues began at Pentecost. Tongues was expected and encouraged by the Apostles. They laid hands on the baptized and non-baptized to receive from the Father, His Holy Spirit and the out pouring of Tongues.

Prayer in Tongues defined:

Praying in Tongues is a prayer in non-vernacular speech (non-native language), which comes from the Holy Spirit.

There are nine common manifestations or Gifts of the Spirit defined in 1 Corinthians:

⁴ There are different kinds of gifts, but the same Spirit distributes them. ⁵ There are different kinds of service, but the same Lord. ⁶ There are different kinds of working, but in all of them and in everyone it is the same God at work. ⁷ Now to each one the manifestation of the Spirit is given for the common good. ⁸ To one there is given through the Spirit a message of wisdom, to another a message of knowledge by means of the same Spirit, ⁹ to another faith by the same Spirit, to another gifts of healing by that one Spirit, ¹⁰ to another miraculous powers, to another prophecy, to another distinguishing between spirits, to another speaking in different kinds of tongues, and to still another the interpretation of tongues. ¹¹ All these are the work of one and the same Spirit, and he distributes them to each one, just as he determines.

1 Corinthians 12: 4-11

From this Scripture passage we see nine common manifestations or Gifts of the Spirit as described by St. Paul. These Gifts are received when we receive the Baptism in the Spirit. In Baptism in the Spirit there is a mutual giving. We give ourselves to the Lord. He gives Himself to us and we become infused with His Holy Spirit.

God the Father wants to give us His Holy Spirit. The Father's gift is *one gift* and that is His Spirit. In the Spirit resides all of the manifestation and much, much more. When you receive the Spirit, you receive **all** of the Spirit.

As well as the nine 1 Corinthian Gifts, there is a list of seven Gifts mentioned in Isaiah 11: 1-3: wisdom, understanding, counsel, fortitude, knowledge, piety, and fear of the Lord. These Gifts are meant to build up the individual.

Again, it is **one Gift**, that being the Holy Spirit. Through the Holy Spirit, nine common charisms[1], or charismatic manifestations are released within us: Tongues, Interpretation of Tongues, Prophecy, Word of Wisdom, Word of Knowledge, Discernment of Spirits, Miracles, Faith and Healing. These are common tools of the Christian used to build the Christian Community.

For Paul the Gift of Tongues is primarily a gift of personal prayer.

> [2] *For anyone who speaks in a tongue does not speak to people but to God. Indeed, no one understands them; they utter mysteries by the Spirit.*
> 1 Corinthians 14: 2

Paul also says, a person praying in Tongues does not understand what he is saying, his mind contributes nothing, but he is nevertheless personally edified by praying in Tongues.

> [4] *Anyone who speaks in a tongue edifies themselves, but the one who prophesies edifies the church.*
> 1 Corinthians 14: 4

The word 'edify' may sound rather pious or self-serving; what is meant is that Tongues builds up the individual because the Spirit is at prayer.

Paul uses adjectives like "desirable" and "edify":

Paul makes it clear that it is desirable to have the Gift of Tongues:

> *⁵I would like every one of you to speak in tongues..."*
> 1 Corinthians 14: 5

Paul is saying that the gift is not just for him but for everyone. He is implying that the Gift of Tongues is desirable and that he wants everyone to speak in Tongues.

And again,

> *⁴Anyone who speaks in a tongue edifies themselves...*
> 1 Corinthians 14: 4

Paul says speaking in Tongues edifies us, lifts us up, connects us, and revitalizes us. Are you feeling worn down, lacking in energy, and spiritual power? The quickest way to re-energize is to begin speaking in Tongues.

When you speak in the Spirit, you are accessing the spiritual realm, your mind is not necessary and gets left behind. You are being lifted up. You are able to leave troubles of this world behind and rest in His Spirit, the Spirit of Peace.

Gradually your mind will catch up and start hearing the thoughts of God. You will gain insight into the troubles and concerns of the world through the Gifts of Wisdom and Understanding.

As we yield to the Gift of Tongues we are learning to speak to God:

> *² For anyone who speaks in a tongue does not speak to people but to God. Indeed, no one understands them; they utter mysteries by the Spirit.*
> 1 Corinthians 14: 2

Paul is saying that those around do not understand us because we are not speaking to them but to God. We are speaking in mysteries by the Spirit. We will speak about the idea of *mysteries by the Spirit* later.

Furthermore, Paul says we speak to God in ways we do not understand. The Spirit helps us in our weakness:

> *²⁶ In the same way, the Spirit helps us in our weakness. We do not know what we ought to pray for, but the Spirit himself intercedes for us through wordless groans.*
> Romans 8:26

Paul has explained the Gift of Tongues is desirable, he wishes everyone to have it, and it edifies the individual.

Furthermore, he explains Tongues is speaking to God and it opens us to the spiritual. As we yield to the Gift of Tongues we are learning to speak to God. Paul says we are speaking in mysteries and that the Spirit will help us.

Yielding to the Holy Spirit:

As Christians we are to be possessed by the Holy Spirit! We are to walk in the Spirit, allowing the Spirit to guide out lives.

Dr. Charles Stanley[2] describes it this way:

> *To walk in the Spirit, is to live moment by moment in dependency upon Him, sensitive to His voice and in obedience to Him.*

Dr. Stanley describes three key words: **Dependent**, **Sensitive** and **Obedient**.

Others have used the word possessed. Possessed by the Holy Spirit means *'yielding'* to the Holy Spirit.

When we invite the Spirit into our body – we yield our bodies to the Holy Spirit. Thus, our bodies become a 'Temple' of the Holy Spirit.

> *[19] Do you not know that your bodies are temples of the Holy Spirit, who is in you, whom you have received from God? You are not your own; [20] you were bought at a price. Therefore honor God with your bodies.*
> 1 Corinthians 6:19-20

The Holy Spirit resides within us. Our body is then a temple for the Holy Spirit. We honor the Spirit and become more sensitive to Him. We become dependent on Him, listening for His direction. We leaning on the direction with an open heart, obedient to His direction in our life.

In the Gifts of the Spirit, we are *yielding* different modalities to the Holy Spirit:

- In Tongues we yield our voice/tongue to the Holy Spirit.
- In Prophesy we yield our mind and voice to the Holy Spirit.
- In Word of Knowledge ad Word of Wisdom we yield our mind and heart to the Holy Spirit.

Yielding is all about allowing the Spirit to direct us and guide us: Dependency, Sensitivity and Obedience.

Tongues is always under the control of the individual:

Tongues is non-vernacular speech from the Holy Spirit, under the control of the individual. Like any speech, if you do not open your mouth and activate the sounds nothing comes out. The same is true with Prophecy. The Prophet has the inspiration but has to then speak out the message using one's voice. Praying or speaking in Tongues is always under the control of the one speaking and can be turned on and off. Intellect is not used.

Here is what some Preachers say about Tongues:

Steve Clark in his book, *Team Manual for Life in the Spirit Seminars* says:

> "Praying in Tongues can build a person's faith in a concrete way. It gives a clear experience of what it means to have the Holy Spirit work through you – an experience of being fully active and yet the Holy Spirit is forming something new through you..."[3]

The practice of surrendering to the Holy Spirit with our tongues, while at the same time co-operating with Him, will increase wisdom in us. Bishop Joseph McKinney[4] from the Diocese of Grand Rapids in Michigan is quoted as saying,

> "Through the Gift of Tongues, I became more sensitive to God's initiatives. Preaching is more powerful when I depend on the power of the Holy Spirit. Prayer is richer when I yield to the Holy Spirit. Ministry is more fruitful when I invoke the Holy Spirit. Building community becomes more important to me when I am sensitive to the Holy Spirit."

We are starting to get a picture that Tongues is an important tool for the Christian. It makes us more sensitive to God's initiatives, makes ministry more powerful, builds community, enriches prayer and we become more whole and more interactive with the triune God.

How does this apply to my life today?

You begin to see that Tongues is a normal requirement in our daily life.

In using the Gift we allow the Lord to take over in our lives. As John the Baptist said:

> ^{30} *He must become greater; I must become less.*
> John 3:30

Or another translation says:

> *He must increase, I must decrease.* KJV

Paul exhorts us to pray in Tongues at all times:

> ^{18}*And pray in the Spirit on all occasions with all kinds of prayers and requests. With this in mind, be alert and always keep on praying for all the Lord's people.*
> Ephesians 6: 18

With Tongues we are praying in the Spirit. It is the Spirit who prays in mysteries unto the Lord. With the Spirit you can discover the exact spot that you need to tackle your problem or situation.

> ^{26} *In the same way, the Spirit helps us in our weakness. We do not know what we ought to pray*

> *for, but the Spirit himself intercedes for us through wordless groans.*
> Romans 8: 26

In Tongues we are speaking to God – mysteries in the spirit.

> *¹Follow the way of love and eagerly desire gifts of the Spirit, especially prophecy. ² For anyone who speaks in a tongue does not speak to people but to God. Indeed, no one understands them; they utter mysteries by the Spirit.*
> 1 Corinthians 14: 1-2

Tongues is praying in the Spirit. In Tongues we are praying Mysteries unto the Lord.

Tongues edifies the individual:

> *³ But the one who prophesies speaks to people for their strengthening, encouraging and comfort. ⁴ Anyone who speaks in a tongue edifies themselves, but the one who prophesies edifies the church.*
> 1 Corinthians 14: 3-4

So then, Tongues is edifying the individual and is building them up. Let's go on:

> *⁵ I would like every one of you to speak in tongues, but I would rather have you prophesy. The one who prophesies is greater than the one who speaks*

> *in tongues, unless someone interprets, so that the church may be edified.*
> 1 Corinthians 14: 5

In this scripture Paul is contrasting the Gifts of Tongues and Prophecy. Therefore Tongues, as well as being a personal prayer language, can also be used as a prophetic gift needing interpretation. Paul is encouraging that both these gifts, Tongues and Prophecy, are available to the Christian and should be normal in their life. Notice he said, "*I would like every one of you to speak in tongues.*" Everyone!

Everyone! That means you!

What Paul is implying is that these Gifts are normal, natural and ordinary in a believer's life. That we, you and I, should be using these Gifts daily on a regular basis and often in our life. He even went on to compare his use of Tongues to those around him:

> *[18] I thank God that I speak in tongues more than all of you.*
> 1 Corinthians 14: 18

From this scripture we can draw the conclusion; that Paul used the Gift of Tongues often throughout the day, that he considered this a normal Gift and was encouraging others to use this Gift to fulfill the direction in Thessalonians:

> *¹⁶ Rejoice always, ¹⁷ pray without ceasing, ¹⁸ give thanks in all circumstances: for this is the will of God in Christ Jesus for you.*
> 1 Thessalonians 5: 16-19

Accessing the Rivers of Living Waters:

> *³⁷ On the last and greatest day of the festival, Jesus stood and said in a loud voice, "Let anyone who is thirsty come to me and drink. ³⁸ Whoever believes in me, as Scripture has said, rivers of living water will flow from within them." ³⁹ By this he meant the Spirit, whom those who believed in him were later to receive. Up to that time the Spirit had not been given, since Jesus had not yet been glorified.*
> John 7: 37-39

Up to this point the Holy Spirit was only seen on and through significant figures in the Old Testament, such as the prophets, Moses and King David. Jesus explains that when He is glorified, the Father will send the Spirit. The Holy Spirit is the Gift from God the Father. Then, and only then, will we able to access the *rivers of living waters*. These rivers will flow from within us; from within our body the Temples of God.

Did you notice that scripture refers to accessing the *"Rivers,"* not one river but many *Rivers of Living Water*. It is not a little guggling stream or trickling brook. It is a river, and not just a river but rivers. In other words, there is an endless supply, *"Let anyone who is thirsty come to me and drink."* All we have to do is believe, *"Whoever believes in me, as Scripture has said, rivers of living water will flow from within them."*

How are you going to get the *rivers of living water flowing from within*? John's Scripture says *let anyone who is thirsty come to me and drink,* and that *living waters will flow from within them* - from their belly, from within.

How are you going to get this living water flowing? You get this living water flowing by praising God and by praying in Tongues! You open to the Spirit by praising God and activating your Tongues, which in turn activates the rivers of living water.

How much of this living water do you want? If you pray for a minute, you get a minute's worth. If you pray for an hour, you get an hours' worth. But what if you pray in Tongues all day, every day?

We are to be charged up! We are to transform the world around us like salt and yeast. You accomplish this by spending time in Tongues, praying for your brothers and sisters in Christ, praying for issues, praying about your neighbor that bothers you, and praying protection for your children.

Do you know how to open the gates of Heaven? Pray in the Spirit! Tongues opens the spiritual realm. It opens us to its mysteries.

> *[2] For anyone who speaks in a tongue does not speak to people but to God. Indeed, no one*

understands them; they utter mysteries by the Spirit.
1 Corinthians 14: 2

An expression of intimacy:

Tongues is an expression of greater intimacy with God. With Tongues we speak to God!!!

God the Holy Spirit, through this Gift that we activate, is using our voice to praise God. As we come to use it, we become more connected, more in tune and more alive in Him.

There is a River of Living Water inside your belly. This River of Living Water is like an atomic bomb that is available anytime you need to release it. It is available to you anytime you need it.

Tongues is used to edify you and to build you up. How do you get built up? Pray in Tongues! When you pray in Tongues, it connects you to the Spirit Realm, to the Living Water.

What about mysteries?

What about your intellect? When you enter into the Spirit your mind catches up, because you start hearing the mind of God through the Word of Wisdom, Word of Knowledge and Prophecy. You start to connect with the Spirit realm and that is where the breakthrough occurs. People want understanding. Through Tongues and opening up to the Spirit, we can receive a breakthrough in the natural. Praying in Tongues opens the door to spiritual things. It opens the door to mysteries. (See the section entitled: *The Spirit will teach us* to learn how mysteries and the Spirit work.)

Summary:

With Tongues you access the supernatural; you edify yourself. When you pray in Tongues there will be evidence that the Spirit of God is upon you, and that you are filled with His power. Tongues moves us from the ordinary to the extra ordinary. The Spirit of God moves us, opening us up to the world where Jesus lives. Jesus was open to Kingdom of God; Tongues opens us to Heaven's blessings.

Do you want to have new ideas? Pray in Tongues! When you pray in Tongues your mind connects to the mind of God, your capacity to receive is increased, you have the capacity to stay longer in prayer, and can communicate longer with God.

Scripture says we do not understand what we are saying. People often say, "I do not understand what I am saying. I am not going to pray in that manner." This is unfortunate, because when we pray in Tongues, we are releasing the *Rivers of Living Water* within us, which proclaim the things of God. The Rivers of Living Water heal, exhort, love and bless. It is not a static event but a potentially tumultuous, explosive, Dunamis power. Tongues opens us up to God's mysteries. (Refer to the section titled, *The Spirit will teach us* or understanding of how mysteries and the Spirit work.)

Did you know that, everything God has for you, is a blessing? The more you apprehend from His Holy Spirit, the more you release the *Rivers of Living Water*, the more you are communing with God and the more you will feel the Fruit of His Spirit – Love, Joy, Peace, Patience, Gentleness and Self Control (Galatians 5: 22-23).

Do you need more Love? Pray in Tongues! Do you need more Joy? Pray in the Spirit! Do you need more Peace, Patience, Gentleness and Self Control? Pray in Tongues!

> *[16] Rejoice always, [17] pray continually, [18] give thanks in all circumstances; for this is God's will for you in Christ Jesus.*
> 1 Thessalonians 5: 16-18

Pray in your Tongues! Tongues empowers the believer!

Section 2 – Depth:

We do not understand, so 'what do we do'?

The scripture has said, when we are praying in Tongues, we do not understand what we are saying. What then do we do?

> *[13] For this reason the one who speaks in a tongue should pray that they may interpret what they*

> *say. ⁱ⁴ For if I pray in a tongue, my spirit prays, but my mind is unfruitful. ¹⁵ So what shall I do? I will pray with my spirit, but I will also pray with my understanding; I will sing with my spirit, but I will also sing with my understanding.*
> 1 Corinthians 14: 13-15

The above scripture is speaking of two approaches. One, we pray in Tongues believing we are communicating with God; this is our active Faith. Next, we pray for interpretation so that we may understand and so that we can pray with our understanding.

The scripture repeats the idea replacing the word pray with sing, *"I will sing with my spirit, but I will also sing with my understanding."* When we sing in the Spirit, we do not have understanding, but Faith. Often the Spirit will give us a song which speaks to our understanding, a song that is familiar to us and touches our heart.

When these things happen, scripture says:

> ¹⁶ *Otherwise, when you are praising God in the Spirit, how can someone else, who is now put in the position of an inquirer, say "Amen" to your thanksgiving, since they do not know what you are saying?*
> 1 Corinthians 14: 16

As we pray in Tongues the Spirit guides the process, giving us first Tongues then natural language or song, so that the inquiring mind can understand and participate in the praise and worship of our God. Also, we can pray that we may *interpret*, again providing for the fruit of understanding. Isn't the Spirit amazing?

The Spirit will teach us:

The Spirit will teach us. The Spirit will lead us to all truth. He is not going to lead us into error. We try to do things on our own. We try to get revelation through our own intellect, but it doesn't work. If you want to access mysteries, if you want to access things that you do not have an answer for, pray in Tongues, asking God to give you a solution. Ask Him to give you an answer. Ask Him to give you instructions.

He wants all of us to act in his name. He wants all of us to speak in new Tongues. In fact, He wants us to do even more than He did.

> *[18] Then Jesus came to them and said, "All authority in heaven and on earth has been given to me. [19] Therefore go and make disciples of all nations, baptizing them in the name of the Father and of the Son and of the Holy Spirit, [20] and teaching them to obey everything I have commanded you. And surely I am with you always, to the very end of the age."*
> Matthew 28: 18-20

And Jesus repeated it even more strongly in the book of John:

> *^{12} Very truly I tell you, whoever believes in me will do the works I have been doing, and they will do even greater things than these, because I am going to the Father.*
> John 14: 12

Jesus says all will heal, all will cast out and to not withhold what you have freely received.

> *^{8} Heal the sick, raise the dead, cleanse those who have leprosy, drive out demons. Freely you have received; freely give.*
> Matthew 10: 8

We are being called to enter into God's Spirit and expand our potential. Everything is available to us through His Spirit. Tongues is just one of the signs of the Spirit given by the Father.

By praying in Tongues, you build yourself up. You have access to the Lord, and you are open to Knowledge and Wisdom. You also expand yourself by opening up to other Gifts and to spiritual activity. Your Tongues effects the atmosphere around you, charging it with God's Glory.

God has answers to the mysteries of mankind. God is above and beyond.

This Spirit you received, is the same Spirit that came over Jesus when He was Baptized (Matthew 3:13-17). It is the same Spirit that hovered over the formless mass when God the Father created the earth (Genesis 1: 2). The Spirit charged Jesus, and in the same way charges you. You have the unimaginable power to preach, cast out demons (Mark 3: 14-15; 6:7-11; 16: 15-18) and to heal (Luke 9: 1-5).

Did you ever come to a situation where you did not know what to do? Have you tried to fix something or solve a problem but do not know what is the source or root of the problem? Pray in Tongues!

Jim Hogan and I did some work with some pre-teens in Rocky Mountain House, Alberta, Canada. We were prompted to ask them; "Can you pray when you are angry?" "No," they responded! It is difficult to pray when you are angry, but you can pray in Tongues. When you kick into Tongues the anger subsides. You can hear more clearly, and you can access the Spirit's understanding. With that wisdom the youngens were able to enter into the Spirit, asking Him to fill them. They received the Baptism in the Spirit.

When you are lonely, pray in Tongues. When you are afraid, pray in Tongues. When you are confused, pray in Tongues and the Spirit will guide you with Gifts of Understanding, Word of Knowledge and Word of Wisdom. The Spirit will open the mysteries of the Lord.

The Spirit is there to move you into the supernatural, there to take you above and beyond, there to have you live the kind of life that Jesus lived. Did He walk in defeat? No! Did He walk in poverty? No! Jesus walked under blessing, under an open Heaven. To a Christian, walking in the Spirit is normal, natural and ordinary.

We are told by Timothy to stir-up the Spirit within:

In the book of Timothy we are told to fan into flame or 'stir-up' the Gift of God which is in you. The Holy Spirit is the Gift from God the Father. The Holy Spirit resides within us, within our temple.

> *^{6} For this reason I remind you to fan into flame the gift of God, which is in you through the laying on of my hands. ^{7} For the Spirit God gave us does not make us timid, but gives us power, love and self-discipline.*
> 2 Timothy 1: 6-7

The Holy Spirit wants to reside within us. Then the Holy Spirit wants to move through us to touch other people. *The Rivers of Living Water* (John 7: 37-39) are given to us to touch other people.

The Study of the Phenomena/Gift of Speaking in Tongues – Glossolalia:

Dr. Andrew Newberg[5] is considered a pioneer in the neuroscientific study of religious and spiritual experiences. He is a faculty member in the Department of Integrative Medicine and Jefferson Medical School. His field is frequently referred to as *neurotheology.* Broadly speaking, neurotheology is a multidisciplinary field of study that seeks to understand the relationship specifically between the brain and theology, and more broadly between the mind and religion.

Dr. Newberg is interested in understanding the relationship between the brain, religion, and health. His research has included brain scans of people in prayer, meditation, rituals, and various trance states. (Newberg, 2006).

At the University of Pennsylvania, Dr. Andrew Newberg has been conducting a scientific study of the phenomenon for a long time. Dr. Newberg found that brain scans show quite different results with Christians praying in Tongues compared to Buddhist monks meditating and Franciscan nuns praying. The frontal lobes—the part of the brain right behind the forehead that's considered the brain's control center—went quiet in the brains of tongue-speakers.

Dr. Newberg is quoted as saying,

> "When they are actually engaged in this whole very intense spiritual practice...their frontal lobes tend to go down in activity. It is very consistent with the kind of experience they have, because they say that they're not in charge. [They say] it's the voice of God, it's the Spirit of God that is moving through them,"
> "Whatever is coming out of their mouth is not what they are purposefully or willfully trying to do. And that's in fairly stark contrast to the people who are—like the Buddhist and Franciscan nuns—in prayer, because they are very intensely focused

and, in those individuals, the frontal lobes actually increase activity."

We can summarize from Newberg's studies that the Gift of Tongues is a God given gift that does not interfere with other brain functions. We know that people can hear, see, think and process while they are praying in Tongues. We know people can read their Bibles while praying in Tongues.

We also know that while using the Gift of Tongues the person is not in control of the Tongue, other than the person can start and stop it at will. The Holy Spirit is using the individual's Tongue to praise God.

The following section outlines more of Dr. Newberg's research.

<u>Decreased Brain Activity</u>: [6]

Glossolalia, otherwise referred to as "speaking in tongues," has been around for thousands of years, and references to it can be found in the Old and New Testament. Speaking in tongues is an unusual mental state associated with specific religious traditions. The individual appears to be speaking in an incomprehensible language yet perceives it to have great personal meaning. Scientists are attempting to explain what actually happens physiologically to the brain of someone while speaking in tongues.

Researchers in the School of Medicine have discovered decreased activity in the frontal lobes, an area of the brain associated with being in control of oneself. This pioneering study, involving functional imaging of the brain while subjects were speaking in tongues, is in the November issue of *Psychiatry Research: Neuroimaging*.

Radiology investigators observed increased or decreased brain activity—by measuring regional cerebral blood flow with SPECT (Single Photon Emission Computed Tomography) imaging—while the subjects were speaking in tongues. They then compared the imaging to what happened to the brain while the subjects sang gospel music.

"We noticed a number of changes that occurred functionally in the brain," comments Principal Investigator Dr. Andrew Newberg, associate professor of radiology, psychiatry and religious studies, and director for the Center for Spirituality and the Mind. "Our brain imaging research shows us that these subjects are not in control of the usual language centers during this activity, which is consistent with their description of a lack of intentional control while speaking in tongues."

Dr. Newberg went on to explain, "These findings could be interpreted as the subject's sense of self being taken over by something else. We, scientifically, assume it's being taken over by another part of the brain, but we couldn't see, in this imaging study, where this took place. We believe this is the first scientific imaging study evaluating changes in cerebral activity—looking at what actually happens to the brain—when someone is speaking in tongues. This study also showed a number of other changes in the brain, including those areas involved in emotions and establishing our sense of self."

Dr. Newberg concludes that the changes in the brain during speaking in tongues reflect a complex pattern of brain activity. He suggests that since this is the first study to explore this, future studies will be needed to confirm these findings in an attempt to demystify this religious phenomenon.

Section 3 – Scripture:

Understanding the Gift of Tongues by studying Scripture:

In the New Testament, when receiving the Holy Spirit, Tongues was common, usual and normal for believers. It was just a part of the experience at the time of their conversion and observable to all who are present.

HOW DOES TONGUES MANIFEST?

I. TONGUES IS A PERSONAL PRAYER:

The following Scriptures give an understanding of Tongues used as a personal prayer language between God and the individual.

Tongues is one of the signs that accompanies believers. Every believer should expect to speak in Tongues.

> *[17] And these signs will accompany those who believe: In my name they will drive out demons; they will speak in new tongues; [18] they will pick up snakes with their hands; and when they drink deadly poison, it will not hurt them at all; they will place their hands on sick people, and they will get well.".*

Mark 16: 17-18

The Gentiles receive the Holy Spirit and begin speaking in Tongues and praising God.

> *[44] While Peter was still speaking these words, the Holy Spirit came on all who heard the message. [45] The circumcised believers who had come with Peter were astonished that the gift of the Holy Spirit had been poured out even on Gentiles. [46] For they heard them speaking in tongue and praising God.*

Acts 10: 44-46

The Holy Spirit came on them and they spoke in Tongues.

> *[1] While Apollos was at Corinth, Paul took the road through the interior and arrived at Ephesus. There he found some disciples [2] and asked them, "Did you receive the Holy Spirit when you believed?" They answered, "No, we have not even heard that there is a Holy Spirit." [3] So Paul asked, "Then what baptism did you receive?" "John's baptism," they replied. [4] Paul said, "John's baptism was a baptism of*

> *repentance. He told the people to believe in the one coming after him, that is, in Jesus." ⁵ On hearing this, they were baptized in the name of the Lord Jesus. ⁶ When Paul placed his hands on them, the Holy Spirit came on them, and they spoke in tongues and prophesied. ⁷ There were about twelve men in all.*
> Acts 19: 1-7

The Spirit helps us in our weakness interceding in sighs too deep for words.

> *²⁶ In the same way, the Spirit helps us in our weakness. We do not know what we ought to pray for, but the Spirit himself intercedes for us through wordless groans.*
> Romans 8: 26

One who speaks in Tongues speaks to God not to men.

> *² For anyone who speaks in a tongue does not speak to people but to God. Indeed, no one understands them; they utter mysteries by the Spirit.*
> 1 Corinthians 14: 2

If we are speaking in our tongues at the same level as the brothers and sisters around us, praising the Lord in our unknown language, we are living within this Scripture. This would happen when a group of people are praising God in their Tongues.

One who speaks in Tongues edifies himself.

> *⁴ Anyone who speaks in a tongue edifies themselves, but the one who prophesies edifies the church.*
> 1 Corinthians 14: 4

One who prays in Tongues prays in Spirit.

> *¹⁴ For if I pray in a tongue, my spirit prays, but my mind is unfruitful.*
> 1 Corinthians 14: 14

Paul implies he speaks in Tongues often.

> *¹⁸ I thank God that I speak in tongues more than all of you.*
> 1 Corinthians 14: 18

The Ephesians are being told to Pray in the Spirit. Prayer in the Spirit can be done in all types of prayers and requests.

> *¹⁸ And pray in the Spirit on all occasions with all kinds of prayers and requests. With this in mind, be alert and always keep on praying for all the Lord's people.*
> Ephesians 6: 18

II. IS INTERPRETATION NECESSARY?

In the Book of Acts there are a number of references which give light to the question whether interpretation is necessary. Tongues does not necessarily need to be interpreted, although scripture gives us examples of times when listeners know the meaning almost miraculously. There are other times listeners do not understand and times when believers recognize that the people are speaking in Tongues but there is no mention of interpretation.

A. TONGUES CAN BE UNDERSTOOD BY UNBELIEVERS (WITHOUT INTERPRETATION - POSSIBLY A MIRACLE):

All in the Upper Room received the Holy Spirit and spoke in Tongues. People were able to hear a language familiar to them, but not necessarily that the Apostle's and the others in the Upper Room were speaking those languages. There is no mention of interpretation.

All in the Upper Room were speaking in Tongues. Each person heard them in their native language.

> *[1] When the day of Pentecost came, they were all together in one place. [2] Suddenly a sound like the blowing of a violent wind came from heaven and filled the whole house where they were sitting. [3] They saw what seemed to be tongues of*

fire that separated and came to rest on each of them. ⁴ All of them were filled with the Holy Spirit and began to speak in other tongues as the Spirit enabled them.
⁵ Now there were staying in Jerusalem God-fearing Jews from every nation under heaven. ⁶ When they heard this sound, a crowd came together in bewilderment, because each one heard their own language being spoken. ⁷ Utterly amazed, they asked: "Aren't all these who are speaking Galileans? ⁸ Then how is it that each of us hears them in our native language?
Acts 2: 1-8

B. SOME OF THE LISTENERS DID NOT UNDERSTAND TONGUES:

This is explained by the fact, that the listeners thought the Apostles were drunk and speaking in babble (incomprehensible). If the Apostles had been speaking in the languages of the crowd would not scripture have given evidence of the fact?

Accusations that the Apostles had too much wine. Peter states that the Apostles are not drunk.

¹² Amazed and perplexed, they asked one another, "What does this mean?" ¹³ Some, however, made fun of them and said, "They have had too much wine." ¹⁴ Then Peter stood up with the Eleven, raised his voice and addressed the crowd: "Fellow Jews and all of you who live in Jerusalem, let me explain this to you; listen

carefully to what I say. ⁱ⁵These people are not drunk, as you suppose. It's only nine in the morning!
Acts 2: 12-15

C. PETER RECOGNIZES THAT THEY ARE SPEAKING IN TONGUES:

Peter went to the house of Cornelius and found a large gathering of people. As he spoke, he was astonished that the gift of the Holy Spirit was poured out on them, even the Gentiles, for he heard them speaking in Tongues and praising God. There is no inference that the Tongues were understood by Peter or other listeners.

Peter hears them speaking in tongues and praising God. There is no indication of interpretation.

> *⁴⁴While Peter was still speaking these words, the Holy Spirit came on all who heard the message. ⁴⁵The circumcised believers who had come with Peter were astonished that the gift of the Holy Spirit had been poured out even on Gentiles. ⁴⁶For they heard them speaking in tongues and praising God. Then Peter said, ⁴⁷"Surely no one can stand in the way of their being baptized with water. They have received the Holy Spirit just as we have."*
> Acts 10: 44-47

III. TONGUES IS A SIGN FOR NON-BELIEVERS:

As believers we should not be afraid of speaking in Tongues in the presence of unbelievers, because it can be a sign to them.

Tongues a sign for unbelievers, Prophesy for believers.

> *²² Tongues, then, are a sign, not for believers but for unbelievers; prophecy, however, is not for unbelievers but for believers.*
> 1 Corinthians 14: 22

LET'S RECAPITULATE:
Tongues seem to be common, natural and normal for believers; it is just part of their experience of their conversion. It is edifying. Tongues is a personal prayer language between God and the individual. In this form, Tongues does not necessarily need to be interpreted, but other times, almost miraculously, listeners understand. Sometimes it is a sign for unbelievers. When you pray in Tongues there will be evidence that the Spirit of God is on you, and you are filled with His power. Tongues opens you to the other Gifts; accessing Knowledge, Wisdom, Discernment and mysteries of God.

- **1 Corinthians 14: 2** – *"For anyone who speaks in a tongue does not speak to people but to God."* Tongues is a personal prayer.
- **1 Corinthians 14: 2** – *"Indeed, no one understands them;"* His mind contributes nothing.

- **1 Corinthians 14: 2** – *"They utter mysteries by the Spirit."* The Spirit is praying mysteries.
- **1 Corinthians 14: 4** – *"Anyone who speaks in a tongue edifies themselves."*
  Edify means constructive building of personality.
- **Romans 8: 26** – *"In the same way, the Spirit helps us in our weakness. We do not know what we ought to pray for, but the Spirit himself intercedes for us through wordless groans."* The Holy Spirit uses our Gift of Tongues to pray to God the Father

---

IV. THE GIFT OF TONGUES USED IN AN ASSEMBLY:

The Gift of Tongues used in an Assembly, as prophesy, needs an interpretation.

DESIRABLE:

1 Corinthians 14: 5-6 – Paul would like everyone to speak in Tongues.

> *⁵ I would like every one of you to speak in tongues, but I would rather have you prophesy. The one who prophesies is greater than the one who speaks in tongues unless someone interprets, so that the church may be edified. ⁶ Now, brothers and sisters, if I come to you and speak in tongues, what good will I be to you, unless I bring you some*

revelation or knowledge or prophecy or word of instruction?

1 Corinthians 14: 12-13 – Pray that you may interpret.

^{12} So it is with you. Since you are eager for gifts of the Spirit, try to excel in those that build up the church. ^{13} For this reason the one who speaks in a tongue should pray that they may interpret what they say.

ORDERLY:

1 Corinthians 14: 27-28 – Speak one at a time.

^{27} If anyone speaks in a tongue, two—or at the most three—should speak, one at a time, and someone must interpret. ^{28} If there is no interpreter, the speaker should keep quiet in the church and speak to himself and to God.

1 Corinthians 14: 39-40 – Done in a fitting and orderly way.

^{39} Therefore, my brothers and sisters, be eager to prophesy, and do not forbid speaking in tongues. ^{40} But everything should be done in a fitting and orderly way.

EDIFIES:

1 Corinthians 14: 5 – Interpreting Tongues Edifies the Church.

> *⁵ I would like every one of you to speak in tongues, but I would rather have you prophesy. The one who prophesies is greater than the one who speaks in tongues, unless someone interprets, so that the church may be edified.*

The purpose of the Prophetic Gift of Tongues in Assembly is to edify the church. It is desirable and is to be done in good order with interpretation.

V. Summary of the manifestation of Tongues:

There are two forms of the Gift of Tongues: A Personal Prayer Gift and a Prophetic Gift.

<u>Personal Prayer Gift</u>: Tongues used as a personal prayer is a gift of prayer from the Holy Spirit for the individual. It is a prayer between the individual and God. It edifies, builds up, the individual. It opens the individual to the other Charismatic Gifts. Most often the individual does not understand what they are saying, their mind does not contribute. The Holy Spirit uses their tongue to pray and praise God.

<u>Prophetic Gift of Tongues</u>: Tongues used in an assembly when everyone is quiet, "speak one at a time", is what we call Prophetic Tongues and is a message from God to His people. We are told that a person with this gift should pray that he may interpret what he says. This gift is meant to edified the church.

Section 4 – Conclusions:

Common Misconceptions:

Over time there have been a number of misconceptions about Tongues and use of Tongues. Let's look a few of the common statements:

Tongues is evidence of the Baptism in the Spirit. Partially True

Here is a quote from a book by Thomas Roycroft[7] that went out of print, and I had the opportunity to republish and edit it.

Quotation from *You Can Minister Spiritual Gifts*:

"The ONLY Holy Ghost baptism is the baptism accompanied by the supernatural experience of SPEAKING IN OTHER TONGUES. This is the Bible standard and it changes not.

Tom Roycroft was quite clear in his writing and preaching, that Tongues was the only clear evidence of the Baptism in the Spirit. This conclusion led him and others of his time to conclude 'no Gift of Tongues – no Baptism in the Spirit'. This Editor has found this to be *inaccurate*.

Tom explained his argument as follows: The disciples before the day of Pentecost had experienced manifestations of faith or miracles or supernatural revelation. Nevertheless, they had not been filled with the Holy Ghost. How do we know? Because Jesus, after He rose from the dead, told them to WAIT until they received the baptism of the Holy Spirit. Therefore, signs, healings, preaching, casting out devils and Divine revelations cannot be regarded as evidence of the baptism of the Spirit.

Listen to the Word;

> *[4] And they were all filled with the Holy Ghost, and began to SPEAK WITH OTHER TONGUES, as the Spirit gave them utterance.*
> Acts 2:4 KJV

So, there is but one evidence - Tongues. Peter referred to the outpouring of the Spirit as:

> *"THIS which ye now SEE and HEAR".*
> Acts 2:33 KJV

What did they see? People being filled with the Spirit. What did they hear? Tongues. So, speaking in other tongues was the evidence. We read that in the house of Cornelius, the Gentile, it was the speaking in other tongues which convinced Peter and his Jewish brethren.

> *[45] The circumcised believers who had come with Peter were astonished that the gift of the Holy Spirit had been poured out even on*

> *Gentiles.* ^{46} *For they heard them speaking in tongues and praising God. Then Peter said,* ^{47} *"Surely no one can stand in the way of their being baptized with water. They have received the Holy Spirit just as we have."*
> Acts 10: 45-47

And later when Peter returned home, it was this same supernatural phenomenon of speaking in other languages which silenced the objections of the skeptical saints in Jerusalem and convinced them that the Spirit had indeed fallen upon the Gentiles.

Peter said:
> ^{15} *"As I began to speak, THE HOLY SPIRIT CAME ON THEM AS HE HAD COME ON US at the beginning.* ^{16} *Then I remembered what the Lord had said: 'John baptized with water, but you will be baptized with the Holy Spirit.'* ^{17} *So if God gave them THE SAME GIFT, he gave us who believed in the Lord Jesus Christ, who was I to think that I could stand in God's way?"* ^{18} *When they heard this, they had no further objections and praised God, saying, "So then, even to Gentiles God has granted repentance that leads to life."*
> Acts 11: 15-18

Twenty-one years later at Ephesus, the evidence of the baptism of the Holy Spirit was still the same.

> *⁶When Paul placed his hands on them, the HOLY SPIRIT came on them, AND they spoke in tongues and prophesied.*
> Acts 19: 6

Nor did tongues cease with the Apostles. Irenaeus mentions it in the second century, and Augustine wrote as follows in the fourth century, "We still do what the Apostles did when they laid hands upon believers and called down the Holy Ghost upon them. IT IS EXPECTED that converts shall speak in new tongues."

Tom Roycroft concludes that Tongues is clear evidence that someone has received the Holy Spirit, but he went on to make a more definitive statement. To sum up: No tongues, no Holy Ghost baptism. No spiritual gifts, no tools to do the job. No tools to do the job, a job poorly done or not done at all. Experience has shown this conclusion to be *inaccurate*.

Roycroft concluded that one has not received the Holy Spirit, if that person does not have the evidence of Tongues. This Editor has found this not to be true in both my personal experience and my life experiences. It is possible to receive the Baptism in the Holy Spirit and yet Tongues is not activated or blocked.

Roycroft softens this conclusion in this next paragraph.

Because a believer has a good measure of God's Spirit some of the nine spiritual gifts may be present in a measure and may even operate to a limited extent, but a believer cannot - I repeat CANNOT - speak in other tongues unless he has been baptized in the Holy Ghost.

THEN with the FULNESS of the Spirit ALL of the nine spiritual gifts can function in their fullness.

Editor's Conclusions from this discussion:
It is clear that the conclusive evidence of receiving the Baptism in the Spirit is the Gift of Tongues, but this does not preclude the possibility that one might receive other Gifts and be active in other Gifts, such as Knowledge, Wisdom and Discernment and not yet have opened to the Gift of Tongues. This was true in the life of this Editor. I, Kenneth, received the Baptism in the Spirit in 1984, with active Gifts of Word of Knowledge, Word of Wisdom, Prophesy and Discernment of Spirits, yet did not activate the Gift of Tongues until the Summer of 1986, two years later."

End of Quotation.

Tongue can only be used if it is interpreted. False

This misconception derives from a scripture:

> ^{26} *What then shall we say, brothers and sisters? When you come together, each of you has a hymn, or a word of instruction, a revelation, a tongue or an interpretation. Everything must be done so that the church may be built up.* ^{27} *If anyone speaks in a tongue, two—or at the most three—should speak, one at a time, and someone must interpret.* ^{28} *If there is no interpreter, the speaker should keep quiet in the church and speak to himself and to God.*
> 1 Corinthians 14: 26-28

This section of the scripture in the NIV is titled "Good Order in Worship" and is talking about using Tongues in an Assembly when everyone is quiet, "speak one at a time". This form of Tongues is what we call Prophetic Tongues and is a message from God to His people. The confusion in the false statement "*Tongue can only be used if it is interpreted,*" is that there are two major forms of Tongues, Tongues used as a personal pray or praise in assembly and Tongues used in the quiet of an assembly as a Prophetic Tongues needing interpretation.

God will give Tongues to me when he wants. Partially True

People who do not receive the gift immediately often make the statement *"God will give it to me when He wants"* or that "they are not worthy," or that "it is not for them." These are rationalizations that people make in an attempt to explain or justify their behaviors. This does not line up with God's Word.

This scripture that best explains God's truth, that He wants us to have all His blessings, is that if we ask, we will receive.

> *^{14} This is the confidence we have in approaching God: that if we ask anything according to his will, he hears us. ^{15} And if we know that he hears us— whatever we ask—we know that we have what we asked of him.*
> 1 John 5: 14-15

God the Father wants to give us His Holy Spirit. The Father's gift is *one gift* and that is His Spirit. In the Spirit resides all of the manifestation including: Healing, Courage, Miracles, Fortitude, Tongues and Prophecy, and much, much more. When you receive the Spirit, you receive all of the Spirit.

It has often been described in this way. Often people receive the Spirit like they might have received a wrapped present. They take the present home and it sits on the mantle, but it is wrapped, unopened. They have still received the Spirit but have not accessed His potential. There needs to be a desire to receive the fullness of the Spirit. Prayer is needed to activate the Spirit.

We are reminded to ask, seek, and knock:

> [7] "Ask and it will be given to you; seek and you will find; knock and the door will be opened to you. [8] For everyone who asks receives; the one who seeks finds; and to the one who knocks, the door will be opened.
> Matthew 7: 7-8

My encouragement to folks who do not immediately receive is to ask again, again, and again. Like the widow in Luke 18: 1-8, who with persistence kept coming to the judge with her plea. God will answer us.

Tongues only occurs by inspiration.
Partially True

This statement suggests that Tongues only occurs when the Holy Spirit overpowers someone and they erupt with

Tongues - inspiration. Now this certainly was true at Pentecost when the tongues of fire came on the Apostles, and they could be heard speaking in Tongues. But it is not proven by other statements in scripture nor by the experiences found in the Charismatic Renewal.

Mark 16:17-18 – Tongues is one of the signs that accompany one who believes. – Every believer should expect to speak in tongues.

> *17 And these signs <u>will</u> accompany those who believe: In my name they <u>will</u> drive out demons; they <u>will</u> speak in new tongues; 18 they <u>will</u> pick up snakes with their hands; and when they drink deadly poison, it <u>will</u> not hurt them at all; they <u>will</u> place their hands on sick people, and they <u>will</u> get well.* (Emphasis added.)

This scripture does not say perhaps, nor does it say possibly, sometimes, could, often, likely, may, nor does it say some get it and some don't. It says will.

> *17 And these signs <u>will</u> accompany those who believe: In my name they <u>will</u> drive out demons; they <u>will</u> speak in new tongues; . . . 18...they <u>will</u> place their hands on sick people, and they <u>will</u> get well.*

Here is another Scripture:

It describes the Upper Room, when the Holy Spirit came at Pentecost. <u>All</u> received the Holy Spirit and Spoke in Tongues.

Acts 2: 1-8 – All speaking in Tongues.

> *¹ When the day of Pentecost came, they were <u>all</u> together in one place.*

Who was gathered? We don't know for sure. They were the Apostles, probably their friends and family.

> *² Suddenly a sound like the blowing of a violent wind came from heaven and filled the whole house where they were sitting.*
> *³ They saw what seemed to be tongues of fire that separated and came to rest on each of them.*
> *⁴ <u>All</u> of them were filled with the Holy Spirit and began to speak in other tongues as the Spirit enabled them.*

ALL OF THEM received the Holy Spirit. ALL OF THEM spoke in Tongues.

Finally let's look at Acts 10 where Peter is preaching:

Acts 10:44-46 – Gentiles receive the Holy Spirit and begin Speaking in Tongues and Praising God.

> *⁴⁴ While Peter was still speaking these words, the Holy Spirit came on <u>all</u> who heard the message.*
> *⁴⁵ The circumcised believers (Jews) who had come with Peter were astonished that the gift of the Holy Spirit had been poured out even on the Gentiles.*
> *⁴⁶ For they heard them speaking in tongues and praising God.*

Note, Peter was preaching when this happened. There was no laying-on of hands. It is an example of the Holy Spirit coming down on people. And note, people were aware this phenomenon had occurred.

The Gift of Tongues has ceased. False

The Bible says the spiritual Gift of Tongues (or languages) will cease. What is not so clear from the Scriptures is when this particular Gift will or did stop.

Many Christians believe this Gift of Tongues stopped after the apostles' death and the completion of the New Testament documents. People who hold this belief are called cessationists because they teach that the gifts including Tongues have ceased. On the other side of the debate are the continuationists who believe that the miraculous gifts have continued.

The passage they struggle with comes from Paul's treatise on Love:

> *[8] Love never fails. But where there are prophecies, they will cease; where there are tongues, they will be stilled; where there is knowledge, it will pass away.*
> 1 Corinthians 13: 8

The primary question Christians fight to answer is, what is the 'completeness', or as found in other translations 'the perfect time,' Paul is talking about?

> ^{9} For we know in part and we prophesy in part, ^{10} but when completeness comes, what is in part disappears.
> 1 Corinthians 13: 9-10

The majority of pastors and theologians agree the Gift of Tongues will pass away when the time of completeness comes. We have found and we believe the Gift of Tongues is active right now and will remain until Christ's second coming. This is when we will see Jesus, face to face as described in the next verse. All need for spiritual gifts like Tongues, Prophecy, and special knowledge will then pass away.

> ^{12} For now we see only a reflection as in a mirror; then we shall see face to face. Now I know in part; then I shall know fully, even as I am fully known.
> 1 Corinthians 13: 12

None of the Gifts will be necessary anymore because we will be in the presence of God.

The Gift of Tongues is not for every believer! False

The idea that the Gift of Tongues in not for everyone comes from the following scripture:

> ^{28} And God has placed in the church first of all apostles, second prophets, third teachers, then miracles, then gifts of healing, of helping, of guidance, and of different kinds of tongues. ^{29} Are all apostles? Are all prophets? Are all teachers?

> *Do all work miracles? ^{30}Do all have gifts of healing? Do all speak in tongues? Do all interpret?*
> 1 Corinthians 12: 28-30

The implied answer to these questions is "no."

But in 1 Corinthians 12-14, Paul outlines the best use of spiritual gifts in the church. He points out problematic situations and offers guidelines to correct their poor use of spiritual gifts. In 1 Corinthians 12: 7, Paul states that the manifestations of the Spirit are for the common good. He equates the body of Christ to a physical body. To be healthy and whole, we need all the parts functioning properly together. With this in mind, Paul tells us that when we come together as a church, everyone should bring a variety of gifts for the common good. In this sense, not everyone will bring a Gift of Tongues, but this does not imply that everyone does not receive the gift.

Paul told the church in Corinth, "*I would like every one of you to speak in tongues*" (1 Corinthians 14: 5), implying that he expected that this would be normal, natural and ordinary for believers to speak in tongues.

Mark also states quite clearly that Tongues is for everyone:

> *^{17}And these signs will accompany those who believe: In my name they will drive out demons; they will speak in new tongues;*
> Mark 16:17

These scriptures are clear, that the statement, *"the Gift of Tongues is not for every believer"* is false. It was expected that those who have been Baptized in the Spirit would receive and use the Gift of Tongues.

Tongues is just gibberish; they are making it up or imitating. This statement is poorly thought out.

It seems to be human nature that we tend to criticize what we don't understand. To gain some understanding let us look at this quotation from Fr. Robert DeGrandis' book *The Gift of Tongues*[8]:

> "As far as making it up, I challenge anyone to stand up and imitate Tongues for five minutes. You can't make it up for any length of time, as it would grate on your human spirit as being 'nonsense'. But when you hear genuine Praying in Tongues it is soothing. The way one can tell is through the Charismatic Gift of Discernment, which is an intuitive gift revealing what is a movement of the Holy Spirit."

One more point in this argument Fr. DeGrandis expressed, challenges us to consider the intent:

> "One more important point I would like to mention is the reflex principle of theology. Every action is determined by its intention. If your intention is to praise God and you are making it up, you are still praising God. If your intention is to praise God and you are imitating someone else, you are still praising God. If your intention is to

praise God and you are making a fool of yourself, you are still praising God. 'God does not see as man sees; man looks at appearances but Yahweh looks at the heart' (1 Samuel 16: 7b)."

SUMMARY:

Tongues is received when the Holy Spirit comes on people.
We call this Baptism in the Spirit.
Tongues is a common experience and is to be expected.
Mark says these signs will accompany those who believe.
Tongues is yielding our gift of speech to the Holy Spirit.
We have come to know that Gift of Tongues is normal, ordinary and expected.

I CHALLENGE YOU!

- Use your Tongues:
  - See how it effects your life.
  - See how it effects the world around you.

- Your Tongues is a Tool. When you first pick up an axe or skill-saw, you are not very efficient and coordinated. You have to learn to use a tool. The same goes with Tongues, it is a tool and you have to learn how to use it.

- A question or two that you might ask:
  - What is the purpose of my Gift of Tongues?
  - Why did God give it to me?
  - How might I use it?

➢ Tongues unleashes the other gifts. It is the <u>Gateway Gift</u>. We have found that Tongues opens up the opportunity for other Gifts to work in our lives. What other Gifts is God offering you?

A PRAYER FOR THE HOLY SPIRIT AND THE GIFT OF TONGUES:

> *Lord, open me to your Holy Spirit.*
> *Holy Spirit, come into my life and dwell in my temple (my body).*
> *Lord, release in me now the Gift of Tongues that I may praise you.*
> *I welcome you and all your Gifts in my life!*

God Bless you. Enjoy your Gift of Tongues.

APPENDIX A

PRAYER FOR BAPTISM IN THE SPIRIT [9]

1. PRAYER FOR EXPECTANT FAITH

LORD, GIVE ME NOW A DEEPER FAITH AND TRUST IN YOU. DEEPEN MY FAITH, LORD. HELP ME TO CLING TO YOU, CLOSER THAN EVER BEFORE. I BELIEVE LORD, THAT YOU LOVE ME AND WANT TO TOUCH ME.

2. PRAYER FOR REPENTANT HEART

HEAVENLY FATHER IN YOUR PRESENCE AND IN THE PRESENCE OF MY BROTHERS AND SISTERS. I ACKNOWLEDGE MY SINS. I REPENT OF MY EVIL WAYS AND ASK FOR YOUR MERCY. IN THE POWER OF THE BLOOD OF JESUS, PURIFY ME AND CLEANSE ME. I FIRMLY RESOLVE WITH YOUR HELP, NEVER TO SIN AGAIN AND TO AVOID WHATEVER LEADS TO SIN. IN THE NAME OF JESUS HAVE MERCY ON ME.

3. PRAYER FOR A FORGIVING HEART

HEAVENLY FATHER, AS YOU HAVE FORGIVEN ME, SO OUGHT I TO FORGIVE THOSE WHO HURT ME. FROM THE DEPTH OF MY HEART, I FORGIVE AND RELEASE TO YOU_____ *(List the name(s) of those who hurt you in the past.)*

4. ACCEPTING JESUS AS LORD

LORD JESUS, I ACCEPT YOU AS MY PERSONAL LORD AND SAVIOR. I PLACE YOU ON THE THRONE OF MY LIFE. I SURRENDER MY LIFE TO YOU. FROM NOW ON I BELONG TO YOU. I WANT TO WALK IN YOUR WAYS AND UNDER YOUR LORDSHIP ALL THE DAYS OF MY LIFE.

5. YIELDING TO THE BAPTISM IN THE SPIRIT

LORD JESUS, NOW I AM READY. I HAVE EMPTIED MYSELF, REPENTED OF MY SINS AND PROCLAIMED YOU AS MY PERSONAL LORD AND SAVIOR. I ASK YOU TO FILL ME WITH THE LIVING WATERS OF YOUR SPIRIT. I CLAIM THE PROMISE YOU MADE, IF WE ASK, WE WILL RECEIVE. I AM NOW ASKING LORD, IN FAITH. COME HOLY SPIRIT AND BAPTIZE ME.

6. PRAYER FOR THE GIFT OF TONGUES

HOLY SPIRIT, PLEASE RELEASE IN ME NOW THE GIFT OF TONGUES. I SURRENDER MY GIFT OF SPEECH TO YOU, SO THAT YOU MAY ENRICH ME WITH A PERSONAL PRAYER GIFT. I ACCEPT YOUR GIVING ME THIS GIFT NOW OR AT A LATER TIME. HOLY SPIRIT ACCEPT THE SYLLABLES I NOW UTTER _____. *(Closing your eyes in tune the word 'Hallelujah', repeating it over and over in expectation.)*

7. PRAYER FOR THE GIFTS

HOLY SPIRIT PLEASE GIVE ME ALL THE OTHER GIFTS THAT YOU SEE FIT, SO THAT I MAY BE EQUIPPED TO LEAD A FULL CHRISTIAN LIFE AND BE OF SERVICE TO THE COMMUNITY. I ASK YOU LORD, TO ENRICH ME WITH THE GIFTS OF WORD OF WISDOM, WORD OF KNOWLEDGE, FAITH, HEALING, MIRACLES, PROPHECY, DISCERNMENT OF SPIRITS, PUBLIC TONGUES, AND INTERPRETATION.

8. THANKSGIVING PRAYER

THANK YOU, JESUS, FOR BAPTIZING ME IN YOUR HOLY SPIRIT. TO YOU BE THE GLORY.

APPENDIX B

Course Material taken from *You Can Minister Spiritual Gifts* (Page 52): [10]

THE GIFT OF TONGUES – 1 Corinthians 12:10

There is speaking in other Tongues, which is A SIGN and there is speaking in other Tongues, which is A GIFT. When it first occurs, speaking in other tongues is a sign that the believer has just been filled with the Holy Spirit; thereafter it continues in the believer's ministry as one of the nine gifts of the Spirit.

In its three aspects tongues is:

1. A SIGN TO UNBELIEVERS
2. A SIGN TO BELIEVERS
3. A GIFT OF THE HOLY SPIRIT

Tongues, as evidence of the supernatural working of God, was a sign to unbelievers on the day of Pentecost. (Acts 2: 11)

Jesus said in Mark 16:17 KJV:

> *"These SIGNS shall follow them that believe . . . they shall speak with new tongues."*

The Apostle Paul, quoting Isaiah 28: 11-12 KJV:

> *"With men of other tongues and other lips will I speak to this people"*

Then he adds,

> *"Wherefore tongues are for a SIGN not to them that believe but for them that believe not."*
> 1 Corinthians 14: 21, 22 KJV

But tongues is also AN EVIDENCE to the believer that God has just filled with the Holy Spirit. Jesus had said to the disciples,

> *"Tarry ye . . . until ye be endued with power from on high."*
> Luke 24: 49 KJV

Then on the day of Pentecost when the disciples had all spoken simultaneously in other tongues, Peter by way of explanation declared,

> *"God hath shed forth this (the gift of the Holy Ghost) which you now SEE and HEAR"*
> Acts 2: 33 KJV

It is apparent from Acts 10: 45-46 that tongues is THE SIGN and EVIDENCE of the baptism of the HOLY GHOST.

> *45 The circumcised believers who had come with Peter were astonished that the gift of the Holy Spirit had been poured out even on Gentiles. 46 For they heard them speaking in tongues and praising God.*
> Acts 10: 45-46

In this course, however, we must mainly concern ourselves with tongues as one of the gifts of the Spirit.

THE GIFT OF TONGUES IS THE GOD GIVEN ABILITY WHICH ENABLES A BELIEVER TO SPEAK AT WILL IN A LANGUAGE WHICH HE DOES NOT KNOW.

The purpose of the gift of tongues is TO EDIFY THE CHURCH when accompanied by interpretation and TO EDIFY THE INDIVIDUAL CHRISTIAN when he speaks in tongues in his private devotions.

To edify means "to build up, to strengthen". It is your spirit which is edified. Paul desired above all things that we might "be strengthened WITH MIGHT by His Spirit IN THE INNER MAN". (Ephesians 3:16 KJV) Speaking much in tongues will do this. We know that the Word of His Grace, the written Word will build us up (Acts 20:32), but too many neglect to make use of this other means of edification, speaking in tongues.

Note that the word "tongues" is in the plural in 1 Corinthians 12:10 and 14:18. The Gift of Tongues is not the ability to speak one language but many.

Sometimes God uses a message in tongues to convey a message to someone present. To him it is not a message in tongues, but a prophecy in his own language.

As we read the Scriptures, we realize the IMPORTANT PLACE WHICH IS GIVEN TO THE HUMAN SPIRIT. It is the spirit of man which is born again, a new creature regenerated by the Spirit of God. It is man's spirit which is indwelt and filled by the Holy Spirit.

When tongues was a sign on the Day of Pentecost, they all spoke simultaneously and there was no interpretation of what was said (Acts 2). In the church service, however, when edification is the object, two or three are to exercise the gift each IN HIS TURN and to be in Divine order there MUST be interpretation after each message in tongues. (1 Corinthians 14: 27) If you do not as yet interpret and you know that there is no one present to interpret then do not give a message in tongues. Paul is not trying to hinder the moving of the Spirit in services but is suggesting that due order and balance be kept in mind. Have you ever noticed, three interpretations and three prophecies will IN GENERAL provide the right proportion of inspired utterance for MOST services.

NOTE ESPECIALLY THE EMPHASIS WHICH THE BIBLE PLACES ON THE SPIRIT OF MAN IN THIS MATTER OF SPEAKING IN TONGUES.

THE BENEFITS OF SPEAKING IN TONGUES:
(*You Can Minister Spiritual Gifts*, Page 55.)[11]

1. MY SPIRIT IS EDIFIED. (1 Corinthians 14: 4). The word edified, or built up, conveys with it the thought of being enlightened, thrilled, blessed, encouraged, strengthened, developed and caused to grow up and mature.

2. MY SPIRIT COMMUNES and has fellowship with God. "In the spirit (His Spirit joined to my spirit) I speak mysteries" (or "Divine secrets", as the Weymouth translation renders it) (1 Corinthians 14: 2). Thus are "the deep things of God" revealed to the spirit of man, explaining spiritual realities with Spirit-taught words, not to his understanding only. (1 Corinthians 2: 10-16).

3. MY SPIRIT PRAYS and, most important of all, prays ACCORDING TO THE WILL OF GOD. (1 Corinthians 14: 14,15; also read Romans 8: 26,27) I can pray with the understanding and sometimes not receive because I am not asking according to the will of God, but when I pray in another tongue I am ALWAYS asking in the will of God. To pray thus is to always receive. Read 1 John 5: 14, 15. Moreover, when my spirit prays in tongues the Holy Ghost causes me to pray for THINGS WHICH OUGHT TO BE PRAYED FOR but which no one thinks to pray for or knows about. Thus, needs known only to God are taken care of. The Bible calls this kind of praying "supplication in the Spirit" (Ephesians 6: 18 KJV) and "praying in the Holy Ghost" (Jude 1: 20).

Tongues is a form of prayer and a much neglected one. Tongues is a way to pray when the mind is perplexed.

4. MY SPIRIT WORSHIPS (John 4:23, 24 and Philippians 3:3). Here is true worship in spirit and in truth, the kind of worship which God seeks for.

5. When in the midst of Satanic opposition and I speak in other Tongues, the Holy Spirit somehow causes MY SPIRIT to be projected in its influence right into the unseen world where the real conflict is going on. Instead of being a distant spectator one seems to be an actual participant enforcing the victory of Calvary on the enemy.

The weapon of victory is the Sword of the Spirit, the word of God going forth from the mouth whether in a known or in an unknown tongue. These were the kind of conflicts with which Paul was familiar. (Ephesians 6:10-18; 2 Corinthians 10:3-5; Colossians 2:1).

6. MY SPIRIT GIVES THANKS to God in another language and, according to 1 Corinthians 14:17, "gives thanks well."

7. The Gift of Tongues enables MY SPIRIT TO SING IN OTHER TONGUES unto the Lord (1 Corinthians 14:15). Sometimes the Spirit of God moves upon an entire congregation and the people break forth into singing in the Spirit like a great heavenly choir, some in English, some in other tongues, and all in perfect harmony. The blessing upon all and the sense of the presence of God is tremendous at such times. Apart from

God such a thing is unexplainable and wholly IMPOSSIBLE.

8. MY SPIRIT WILLS the instant operation of the gift. By an act of my will, I CAN SPEAK IN OTHER TONGUES AT ANY TIME. This is in agreement with 1 Corinthians 14:15 KJV: "I WILL pray with the spirit AND WILL PRAY with the understanding also." Because this gift can be brought into operation at will, the believer can avail himself of needed help without delay. Speaking in tongues is the most important thing one can do to feed, build up and strengthen the spirit. It is a 'QUICK CHARGE' of gigantic power and permanent benefit. It "STRENGTHENS WITH MIGHT IN THE INNER MAN" (Ephesians 3:16 KJV). Paul that spiritual stalwart said:

> *"I thank God I speak in tongues more than ye all."*
> 1 Corinthians 14:18 KJV

9. There is some relation between the WELL-BEING OF THE SPIRIT and THE WELL-BEING OF THE BODY. (3 John 2). "A joyful heart (spirit) doeth good like a medicine" (Proverbs 17: 22 KJV). I have many times observed that the practice of speaking in Tongues which builds up and strengthens the spirit has at the same time the effect of giving new life to the body. Faith is built up and released so that the Holy Spirit has greater liberty to move throughout the mortal body and quicken it. (Romans 8:11)

If you do not speak in Tongues in your daily prayer life it indicates that:

1) You do not really appreciate THE VALUE of it.

2) Or else, you do not understand how this gift operates. Realize this: God does not do the speaking; YOU DO THE SPEAKING. In Acts 2: 4 we read "ALL OF THEM were filled with the Holy Spirit and began to speak in other tongues as the Spirit enabled them."

If you do not find it easy to speak in other Tongues, first throw yourself with ENERGY into praising God in a LOUD VOICE. Then commence to speak in tongues.

To stir up the other gifts of the Spirit within you, throw yourself with energy and emphasis into speaking in another tongue. GIVE YOURSELF WHOLLY TO SPEAKING. The more intense the giving the greater will be the power and blessing and revelation of the Spirit within you and the more effective will be the operation of the other gifts. By speaking in other Tongues, you move more readily into the realm of the Spirit.

Sometimes when you are praying for the sick and afflicted, you find that you have come against some stubborn thing that will not move. Minister in Tongues, for tongues is the bridge into the unseen world where most Satanic hindrances and opposition are entrenched. As you speak, you enter in more fully and overcome by the sword of the Spirit.

NOTES:

[1] Definition: 'Charismatic' from the root charisma or charism, plural charisma or charisms, (Greek – favor, gift; French – grace), as an extraordinary power (as of healing) given to a Christian by the Holy Spirit for the good of the church.
G. & C. Merriam Company. (1963). Charismatic. In Webster's Seventh New Collegiate Dictionary, (7th ed., p. 140).

[2] Dr. Charles Stanley (1932-2023) was Pastor Emeritus of First Baptist Church in Atlanta, Georgia where he served as senior pastor for 49 years. He was the founder and president of In touch Ministries, which widely broadcasts his sermons through television and radio.

[3] Clark, Steve. *Team Manual for Life in the Spirit Seminars,* Servant Publications, Ann arbor, Michigan, U.S.A. 1980.

[4] Bishop Joseph McKinney (1928 – 2010) was a bishop and auxiliary bishop in the Catholic Church serving in the Diocese of Grand Rapids, Michigan from 1968-2001.

[5] Dr. Andrew Newberg is an Associate Professor in the Department of Radiology and Psychiatry and Adjunct Assistant Professor in the Department of Religious Studies.
http://www.andrewnewberg.com

[6] University of Pennsylvania Almanac, 'Journal of Record, Opinion and News', *November 7, 2006, Volume 53, No. 11*
http://www.upenn.edu/almanac/volumes/v53/n11/rr.html

[7] Roycroft, Thomas W. & Kenneth L. Fabbi *You Can Minister Spiritual Gifts,* Kenneth Fabbi, Canada, 2019.

[8] DeGrandis, Robert, *The Gift of Tongues,* 1983. (Out of print). Fr. Robert DeGrandis (1932-2018) was a member of the Society of St. Joseph. As a priest for 59 years, he was involved in leadership training and healing ministry around the world within the Catholic Charismatic Renewal and was a founding member of the Association of Christian Therapists.

[9] The *Prayer for Baptism in the Spirit* is taken from material used by Our Lady of the Assumption Prayer Community, Lethbridge, Alberta, Canada.

[10] Roycroft, Thomas W. & Kenneth L. Fabbi. *You Can Minister Spiritual Gifts*, Kenneth Fabbi, Canada, 2019 – Course Material taken from *You Can Minister Spiritual Gifts*, page 52.

[11] Ibid., page 55.

www.ingramcontent.com/pod-product-compliance
Lightning Source LLC
Chambersburg PA
CBHW071033080526
44587CB00015B/2594